LOS PENITENTES

A BRIEF HISTORY

LOS PENITENTES

A BRIEF HISTORY

by William Farrington

Drawings by Ronald Bayford

THE SUNSTONE PRESS
Santa Fe, New Mexico

Copyright 1975 © By William Farrington

Book and Cover Design: Douglas J. Houston

Cover etching by Will Shuster

Printed in The United States of America

INTRODUCTION

One of the most fascinating, written about, and misunderstood religious groups in the world is *Los Hermanos Penitentes,* a Catholic brotherhood found only in northern New Mexico and southern Colorado. As with all cultures, societies and organizations lacking a written literary tradition, the recorded history of the Penitentes is full of compounded errors and misinterpretations. Legends and folklore, handed down orally over the years, are open to interpretations that are, perhaps, wide of the mark. However, cultural prejudice and bigotry, whether conscious or unconscious, are not more damaging than the overly sympathetic view. It is just as possible to kill with kindness as it is with malice.

The Penitentes have excited interest in travelers to New Mexico for years. The lurid tales of crucifixions, bloody scourgings and sudden death, all accomplished during religious ecstasy, have always appealed to the usually practical Anglo mind. The facts, such as they are, have come from outside observers, scholarly researchers and obvious detractors with a religious bias. Somewhere among all that has been written lies the truth, but since no *hermano* has ever told or written the true story much is still left to conjecture.

From the recorded facts this booklet has been compiled with, it is hoped, some measure of objectivity.

RITUAL

Each Penitente *morada* or chapter is an autonomous entity. It is, therefore, almost impossible to generalize about rites and customs. Some groups emphasize self-flagellation while others rarely make use of the whip. Within a single *morada* it is possible that rituals vary, if not from year to year, at least from generation to generation. But, for the purposes of this pamphlet, we will present a composite of the various ceremonies of the brotherhood.

It must first be understood that *Los Hermanos Penitentes* do not simply appear during Lent and then disband after Easter. They are active benevolent societies given to charitable works throughout the year. They are especially involved at the death of a member during which time they supervise the *velorio* (wake).

When Lent approaches, however, they devote their time to personal and community penance. The members usually meet in the *morada* (the word refers to both the chapter and the meetinghouse) on Wednesdays and Fridays during Lent. Special services are held in preparation for Holy Week which is the most important season of the Church year.

If the penance of self-flagellation is to be performed at any time, the *Sangrador* (bloodletter) makes three slashes on each side of the spine of the penitents with a knife or piece of obsidian. This is also done when a man is initiated into the order. It has generally been assumed that this is a mark or brand of the Penitentes. Actually the gashes allow for the free flow of blood during flagellation and prevent welts, bruises and permanent scars.

Neighboring *moradas* often visit each other during Holy Week in the fulfillment of vows. If there is flagellation it takes place usually on the last three days before Holy Saturday. *La Procesion de Sangre* (Procession of Blood) does not occur as frequently now as it did in the past. The Church has put a ban on public penance of this sort. But in earlier days the Brothers walked from the *morada* to a nearby *Calvario*, a large cross erected on a hill representing Mount Calvary. In this procession the penitents, dressed only in white cotton drawers, whipped themselves with plaited yucca whips called *disciplinas*. The *Pitero* (flute player) played the small *pito* while the Brothers sang *alabados*, very old hymns which are reminiscent of fifteenth and sixteenth-century Spanish songs.

There is always a definite pattern to the procession. The penitents take three steps forward, then toss the *disciplina* over the left shoulder; three steps, over the right shoulder. Because of the gashes the blood flows and soon stains backs, drawers and legs. Some Brothers might carry *maderos*, large wooden crosses, on their shoulders in emulation of Christ. Each penitent has one or two *Acompañadores* (attendants) to help him if he becomes too weak or strays from the path.

On Good Friday *El Encuentro* takes place. This is a service in which women and nonmembers of the *morada* take part. The women carry an image of the Virgin Mary from the village church into the plaza. *Los Hermanos* carry a statue of Christ from the *morada*. The two groups meet and sing *alabados*. This commemorates the meeting of Mary and Jesus on the Via Dolorosa. Sometimes one of the Brothers takes the part of Jesus and carries a large cross.

If there is a crucifixion, it takes place on Good Friday. Here we come to the most controversial part of the Penitente ritual. The actual procedure is quite simple. One Brother is chosen to represent Christ. He is led from the *morada* at the appropriate time, wearing a hood. This is not so much to conceal his identity as to make his penance anonymous and therefore not a matter of pride. Many of the penitents wear masks for the same reason during public processions. The Christ substitute is laid on a large cross and his arms and legs are bound to it with horsehair rope. The cross is then pulled upright and the man hangs there until the ropes cut off circulation, causing unconsciousness. The man is then removed from the cross and taken into the *morada*, where he is revived.

The question will probably always remain: were nails ever used in these crucifixions? There are no authenticated eye-witness reports of nails, but this, of course, does not rule out the possibility. Did anyone ever die from a crucifixion? Again we have no authentic reports. The often repeated legends that a deceased *Cristo's* family was notified of his death by the placing of his shoes on the doorstep appears to be just that — a legend. This is not to say that men have not died on the cross or indeed from a too zealously inflicted self-whipping. The Lenten season in northern New Mexico is usually cold, windy and plagued by frequent snow storms. Physical punishment, loss of blood, and exposure might easily weaken a body enough to cause death. Death, however, is not the aim of *Los Penitentes*. It must be remembered that within the Catholic Church suicide is a mortal sin and the Brothers are seeking to expiate sin, not commit it.

Lacking verifiable instances of crucifixions in which nails were used, we have to make assumptions based on other evidence. Considering Penitente attitudes and practices it is safe to suppose that it probably has happened at some time. But it certainly was never a regular feature of Holy Week activities.

The real climax of the Penitente Holy Week occurs on Good Friday night when *Las Tinieblas* (darkness, confusion, ignorance) is celebrated. This service, based on the Catholic *Tenebrae* reenacts the darkness and confusion that followed Christ's death on the cross. It does not refer to the earthquake of the same period, as many people believe.

Though usually held in the *morada*, this is one service that can be attended by women, children and nonmembers. In front of the altar stands a candelabra holding thirteen candles, representing Christ and his twelve Apostles. *Alabados* are sung and prayers and psalms recited. At the conclusion of each set one candle is extinguished. When the twelve are out, the central candle, the Christ, is removed to an inner room and the *morada* is in total darkness. The Brothers and congregation then break into wailing and screaming and *matracas* (wooden rachets) and chains are rattled. The pandemonium continues while *Los Hermanos*, in another room, apply the *disciplinas* to their backs. Prayers are then said for the deceased. This particular service is not a Penitente innovation. It may also be found in Mexico.

After *Las Tinieblas* Holy Week is ostensibly over for the Brothers. Holy Saturday is very quiet and Easter services are conducted by a priest in the church.

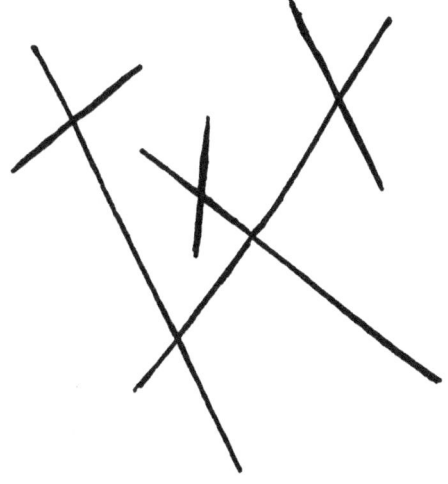

HISTORY

The foregoing gives a brief idea of what the Penitentes do. We now must consider who and what they are. Are the Penitentes all the same even though they are called *Los Penitentes, Los Hermanos de Jesús, La Cofradía, Los Hermanos de Sangre de Cristo* and *Los Hermanos de la Tercer Orden de San Francisco*. The answer is yes and no. In the beginning, and there is still argument over when that was, the various separate groups, called *moradas*, were without formal organization beyond the local level. There were, as far as can be determined, no written rules or supreme body. The groups existed in each village as an entity, and customs, rituals, and rules varied from *morada* to *morada*.

As to those "beginnings," scholars, partisans and detractors clash with such force that it is frequently impossible to tell who is pro and who is con. For the record, let us go back to eleventh-century Europe. During that period flagellanti societies arose, chiefly in central Europe, and were flourishing by the thirteenth century. The Catholic Church never recognized and frequently attempted to suppress these fanatics, often branding them as heretics. Self-flagellation and mutilation are not part of the Roman ethic. Indeed, flagellants who drove themselves beyond endurance and died as a result were considered suicides and denied Church burial.

Though the penalties for flagellanti were strong, societies kept appearing throughout the Middle Ages, especially in times of plague and famine. The Church was never able to suppress them fully. The somber and somewhat emotional religious climate of Spain was ideal for the growth of these penitential groups when the movement found its way there. Though self-flagellation was never the dominant theme of the Spanish societies, it did exist. However, such practices were usually restricted and carried out in strict privacy.

It will probably never be possible to separate facts from the myths of the past. But more recent events are documented. During the 1930's attempts were made at organization. After Archbishop Byrne's statement, some headway was made and the Brotherhoods are now incorporated, nonprofit benevolent associations operating under Church authority. Membership seems to be concentrated in San Miguel, Mora, Taos and Rio Arriba counties in New Mexico and in the San Luis Valley of Colorado. The *Hermanos Mayores* (*morada* leaders) and other representatives meet annually in Santa Fe and are addressed by the archbishop or other church officials.

"PENITENTE WATCHING"

The first question most people ask on learning about the Penitentes is, "Where can I see them in action." The answer is in two parts. 1) Penitente services and processions are held in dozens of small villages in northern New Mexico and southern Colorado each Lent. 2) Unless invited, stay away.

There are hair-raising stories about Penitente guards who carry rifles and shoot first, question later when outsiders get too close. Many are the tales of rock-throwing Brothers who chase tourists down the mountainside hurling invectives with the stones. They are probably all based on truth but it is doubtful that anyone gets shot at anymore. The reason for staying away is that these are religious services of a very private nature and no one likes being gawked at. If, on the other hand, a friend or acquaintance invites you to attend one or more Holy Week observances in a mountain village, by all means go. But go only if you are really interested. It is not an entertainment and should be approached with seriousness and a reverent attitude.

Apologists for the Penitentes of New Mexico usually credit Don Juan de Oñate with bringing the society to New Mexico. This is based almost solely on a mention in Villagra's *History of New Mexico* of Oñate's scourging himself during Holy Week just before entering what is now New Mexico. Self-flagellation was not unknown to these sixteenth-century Spaniards, as we have seen, and it was not uncommon for men to so discipline themselves at Easter, especially if they had not been particularly devout during the preceding year.

It is probably because of this same incident that *Los Penitentes* have for years been assumed to be an off-shoot of the Third Order of St. Francis. St. Francis established his Order in 1221. Shortly thereafter he organized the Poor Clares, an order for women. Because of popular demand he also established a lay order for people who could not take permanent vows. This Third Order was instantly successful and always enjoyed a large membership in Spain. It was brought to the New World by the *Conquistadores* and later found its way to New Mexico with the Spanish settlers. Many historians have assumed the Third Order was slowly corrupted through local practices and evolved into the Penitentes. There is no historical evidence to support this, however.

For that matter, there is no real evidence that connects today's Penitentes with Oñate's Holy Week penance in 1598. There is a long historical blank between the sixteenth century and the next official mention of self-flagellation in New Mexico. Bishop Zubiría in 1833 was the first to object in print to the public penance of Penitente groups. It is a long way from 1598 to 1833. Surely there would have been some mention of these religious excesses if they had been common during that period.

One school of thought claims that no mention was made because the Penitentes as such did not come into being until after 1820. In that year Mexico gained its independence from Spain. The Franciscans who had tended to New Mexico's spiritual needs for over two hundred years were suddenly cut off from the support of the Spanish court. They were, in effect, expelled from Mexican territory. The infant Mexican government had neither the time nor the money to send replacement priests to that lonely frontier. As a result much of northern New Mexico was practically priestless for the next twenty-seven years.

The inhabitants were forced to take over all religious duties, except those specifically assigned to priests. Baptisms, burials and all religious ceremonies and holy days came under the jurisdiction of the local citizens. These people were responsible for keeping the faith alive when it seemed they had been deserted by the Church.

How the flagellation practices became a part of the Penitente rite is not altogether clear. The historical basis did exist and can be traced back to Europe. One thing is certain — it did not come from the New Mexico Indians. Self-flagellation and mutilation have never been an important part of the Southwestern Indian religion. Most of the neighboring Pueblo Indians were horrified at the Spanish bloodletting.

With the coming of the Americans in 1847 many things changed in New Mexico. For one, there was an influx of Anglos, Americans of northern European descent, who were for the most part Protestant. Like the Indians, they were horrified by the Penitentes.

In 1851 New Mexico was given its first Catholic bishop, Jean Lamy, a Frenchman who had served earlier in the eastern United States. His sensibilities were also offended by the Penitente excesses and more than that he feared that they would reflect unfavorably on all Catholics. Which, of course, they did. The pragmatic Yankees did not distinguish between whip-yielding villagers and sophisticated city dwellers. They were all Catholics.

Lamy finally forbade the Holy Week practices under threat of excommunication. It is not known if excommunication was ever invoked, but it did have an immediate effect. The Penitentes, like so many persecuted minorities, did not stop. They simply went underground. Lamy's successor, Archbishop Salpointe, another Frenchman, prohibited all public flagellation and cross-carrying. Those who continued were denied the Sacraments of the Church.

It is probable that the Penitentes would have gone underground anyway. By the late nineteenth century, bigoted Anglos and equally bigoted Spanish-Americans were beginning to make "Penitente watching" a sport. Abuse, ridicule, and attempts to break up processions resulted in increased secrecy. It was during this period that most of the tales of gun-toting *hermanos* firing at tourists came into being.

During the early twentieth century the Brotherhood began to take on a political tone. Just how influential they became at the state level in New Mexico is still unknown. They certainly were able to swing local elections, since in many instances the membership of the Brotherhood practically made up the entire voting public of a number of mountain villages. That they were ever a "Mexican Mafia" is doubtful.

Finally on January 28, 1947, Archbishop Edwin V. Byrne issued a statement concerning the Penitentes. After extolling them for their preservation of the faith during the long periods of neglect, the Archbishop made four major points:

1) The Brotherhood is "a society of men within the Church" and not a fanatical sect outside the Catholic Church.

2) He confirms the opinion that the Penitentes are descendants of the Third Orders founded in New Mexico by the early Franciscans and not of the flagellanti sects of the Middle Ages.

3) The acts of penance are not inspired by sadism or masochism. They must, however, be done in private.

4) If the Brotherhood uses moderation, privacy, and the guidance of the Church, it has the blessing of the Archbishop.

GLOSSARY

Acompañador: attendant, Penitente brother who aids penitents during public processions. From Sp: companion, accompanist.

alabado: a traditional religious hymn. From Sp: to praise.

Calvario: a symbolic Mount Calvary, a large stationary wooden cross visited by Penitentes during Lent and Holy Week.

calzones: white cotton drawers, worn by active penitents

Cofradía: confraternity, often applied to the Penitente Brotherhood.

disciplina: a whip, usually made of yucca fibers, used for self-flagellation.

La Hermandad: The Brotherhood, *Cofradía*.

hermano: brother, used to designate a member of the Cofradía.

Hermano Mayor: Elder Brother, elected leader of a *morada*.

Los Hermanos de Jesús: The Brothers of Jesus, used for Penitentes.

Los Hermanos de Luz: The Brothers of Light, usually refers to initiated members.

Los Hermanos Penitentes: The Penitent Brothers, common name for Penitentes.

madero: Spanish for beam, plank, timber; used to designate large cross dragged by penitents in processions.

matraca: wooden rachet or noisemaker, used especially on Good Friday in place of bells during services.

morada: dwelling, residence; the adobe or stone chapter house of a Brotherhood; also denotes the chapter itself.

Los Penitentes: The Penitents.

Pitero: piper, flute player.

pito: small flute or pipe, played only to accompany religious services. From Sp: whistle.

Rezador: reader, reads or chants parts of Penitente services. From Sp: to pray, to say or recite.

Sangrador: bloodletter, one who makes slashes on backs of initiates and penitents. The slashes allow for the free flow of blood preventing welts from forming during scourging. From Sp: to bleed, to drain, to tap.

Las Tinieblas: darkness, ignorance, confusion. Based on Tenebrae services of the Catholic Church.

BIBLIOGRAPHY

AHLBORN, RICHARD E. *The Penitente moradas of Abiquiú.* Contributions from the Museum of History and Technology, Paper 63 Washington, D.C.: Smithsonian Institution Press, 1968. pp.123-167. Brief history of the Penitentes followed by a discussion of Penitente architecture and artifacts. Good photographs.

ARANDA, CHARLES. *The Penitente papers.* Albuquerque: n.d. 60p. Various documents, rules, constitutions, etc. relating to the Penitentes. Good source book.

CHAVEZ, FRAY ANGELICO. *My Penitente land, reflections on Spanish New Mexico.* Albuquerque: University of New Mexico Press, 1974. 272p. If you are really interested in the subject. No sensationalism. Explodes a lot of myths, beautifully written, intensively researched by one of the Southwest's leading authors.

————. "The Penitentes of New Mexico." *New Mexico Historical Review,* 29(1954):97-123. Concise. Well written and researched.

DE CÓRDOVA, LORENZO. *Echoes of the flute.* Notes by Marta Weigle. Santa Fe: Ancient City Press, 1972. 62p. Personal memoirs of a native of "Penitente Country" who is not himself a Penitente. Worth reading.

DARLEY, ALEXANDER M. *The Passionists of the Southwest, or, The Holy Brotherhood, a revelation of the "Penitentes."* First published in 1893. Glorieta, N.M.: Rio Grande Press, 1968. 119p. Biased and bigoted account by Protestant missionary who hated everything Roman Catholic. However, should be read as a testament of the times. Robert McCoy's excellent appendix is worth the price. Old and new photographs, some never before published.

HENDERSON, ALICE CORBIN. *Brothers of Light, the Penitentes of the Southwest.* Reprint of 1937 edition. Chicago: Rio Grande Press, 1962. 126p. Sensitive, beautifully written. Based in part on personal experiences.

LUMMIS, CHARLES F. *The land of poco tiempo.* First published in 1893. Albuquerque: University of New Mexico Press, 1952. Chapter 4, "The Penitent Brothers," is full of the usual misconceptions and Anglo bias, but it was one of the first (if not the first) Anglo-American descriptions in print. Lummis is slightly less bigoted than Darley. The book is a classic, anyway, and should be read.

MILLS, GEORGE and GROVE, RICHARD. *Lucifer and the Crucifer: the enigma of the Penitentes.* Reprinted from the 1955 *Brand book of the Denver Westerners.* Colorado Springs: Taylor Museum, 1956. 44p. Excellent bibliography. The text is very technical and will appeal to professionals.

WEIGLE, MARTA. *The Penitentes of the Southwest.* Santa Fe: Ancient City Press, 1970. 46p. One of the best surveys for the beginner. Start here.

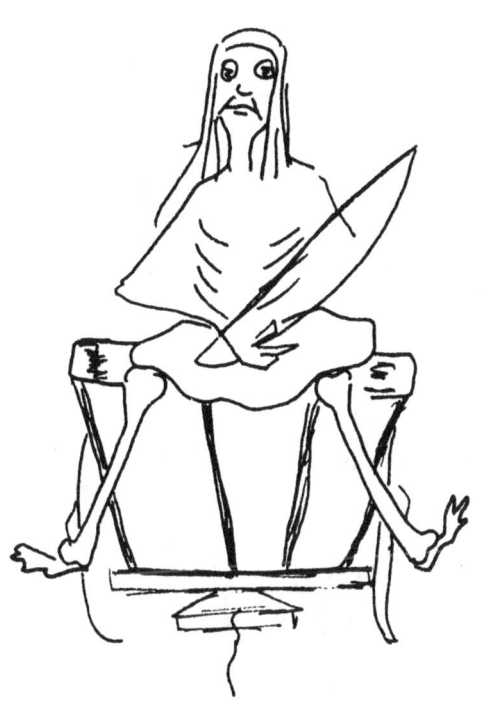

NOTES

NOTES

NOTES

NOTES

www.ingramcontent.com/pod-product-compliance
Lightning Source LLC
Chambersburg PA
CBHW051706040426
42446CB00009B/1329